A Life that Makes a Difference

60-second readings that truly matter

Also by Steve Goodier

One Minute Can Change a Life
Riches of the Heart
Joy Along the Way
Prescription for Peace
Touching Moments
Lessons of the Turtle
The Living Right Side Up Method

Free shipping! Free gift-wrapping!

Please call toll free 1-877-344-0989
Or order from the Web site!
www.LifeSupportSystem.com

Get Steve Goodier's **FREE newsletter**
Your Life Support System.
www.LifeSupportSystem.com

"Sharing Life, Love and Laughter . . ."

A Life that Makes a Difference

60-second readings that truly matter

Steve Goodier

First Edition

Life Support System ♡ Publishing, Inc.
P.O. Box 237 Divide, CO 80814
www.LifeSupportSystem.com

A Life that Makes a Difference

60-second readings that truly matter

By Steve Goodier

Life Support System♡Publishing, Inc.
P.O. Box 237 Divide, CO 80814

Library of Congress Card Number: 2001116662

ISBN 1-929664-22-2 (Soft cover)

Cover design: Brent Stewart & Darrel Voth

Contents

Your Most Valued Strength

I recently learned of a research organization that asked several thousand people, "What are the most serious faults of executives in dealing with their associates and subordinates?" Several could be chosen. What do you think was mentioned most often? Here is the list:

1. 15% Bias and letting emotions rule
2. 15% Indecision
3. 21% Miscellaneous, which includes lack of courtesy, loss of temper, sarcasm, jealousy, nervousness, etc.
4. 17% Failure to delegate authority
5. 17% Arrogance
6. 17% Arbitrariness

7. 19% Lack of frankness and sincerity
8. 24% Lack of leadership
9. 34% Failure to size up employees correctly
10. 36% Failure to show appreciation or give credit
11. 68% Failure to see the other person's point of view

The fault cited most often, as the survey shows, was failure to see the other person's point of view. It was mentioned nearly twice as often as the next most common problem.

Yet on a more positive side, the strength most valued in the workplace is the ability to understand another. And I suspect that strength rates high in all relationships. We don't always need others in our life to agree with us, but we do need to feel heard and understood. In fact, feeling understood may well be one of our greatest emotional needs. Without it, we can feel disheartened, we believe we don't matter, and we find ourselves increasingly unhappy and lonely.

Grade school children demonstrate this important human need to be heard. One writer tells about a group of children who seldom talked about personal problems with their teachers or the school principal for fear of the consequences. But...in which adult were the children confiding most often? The school custodian! Here was a person who would listen without judging. Here was someone safe, someone who would understand.

Author Og Mandino gives us this challenge: "Beginning today, treat everyone you meet as if they were going to be dead by midnight. Extend to them all the care, kindness, and understanding you can muster, and do it with no thought of any reward. Your life will never be the same again."

It's a universal principle: when we habitually decide to be understanding, we soon feel more understood. And our lives are never the same again.

No Regrets

Not many people have heard of Bill Havens. But Bill became an unlikely hero of sorts – at least among those who knew him best. Here is his story:

At the 1924 Olympic Games in Paris, the sport of canoe racing was added to the list of international competitions. The favorite team in the four-man canoe race was the United States team. One member of that team was a young man by the name of Bill Havens.

As the time for the Olympics neared, it became clear that Bill's wife would give birth to their first child about the time that the US team would be competing in the Paris games. In 1924 there were no jet airliners from Paris to the United States, only slow ocean-going ships. And so Bill found himself in a dilemma. Should he go to Paris and risk not being at his wife's side when their baby was born? Or should he withdraw from the team and remain with his family?

Bill's wife insisted that he go to Paris. After all, competing in the Olympics was the culmination of a life-long dream. But Bill felt conflicted and, after much soul-searching, decided to withdraw from the competition and remain home where he could support his wife when the child arrived. He considered being at her side his highest priority – even higher than going to Paris to fulfill his dream.

As it turned out, the United States four-man canoe team won the gold medal in Paris. And Bill's wife was late in giving birth to their child. She was so late, in fact, that Bill could have competed in the event and returned home in time to be with her when she gave birth.

People said, "What a shame." But Bill said he had no regrets. For the rest of his life, he believed he had made the better decision. Bill Havens knew what was most important to him. Not everybody figures that out. And he acted on what he believed was best. Not everybody has the strength of character to say no to something he or she truly wants in order to say yes to something that truly matters. But for Bill, it was the only way to peace; the only way to no regrets. There is an interesting sequel to the story of Bill Havens....

The child eventually born to Bill and his wife was a boy, whom they named Frank. Twenty-eight years later, in 1952, Bill received a cablegram from Frank. It was sent from Helsinki, Finland, where the 1952 Olympics were being held. The cablegram read: "Dad, I won. I'm bringing home the gold medal you lost while waiting for me to be born."

Frank Havens had just won the gold medal for the United States in the canoe-racing event, a medal his father had dreamed of winning but never did. Like I said – no regrets.

Thomas Kinkade eloquently said, "When we learn to say a deep, passionate yes to the things that really matter... then peace begins to settle onto our lives like golden sunlight sifting to a forest floor."

P.S.

I'm so busy I don't know whether I just found a rope or lost my horse.

Fire In The Heart

The teacher quizzed her class: "He drove straight to his goal. He looked neither to the right nor to the left, but pressed forward, moved by a definite purpose. Neither friend nor foe could delay him, nor turn him from his course. All who crossed his path did so at their own peril. What would you call such a man?"

A student replied, "A truck driver!"

If he is a truck driver, he is likely a successful truck driver, for anyone who pursues a vision with such passion is sure to be a success.

Holocaust survivor Elie Wiesel got it right when he said:

The opposite of love is not hate,
it's indifference.
The opposite of art is not ugliness,
it's indifference.

The opposite of faith is not heresy,
it's indifference.
And the opposite of life is not death,
it's indifference.

Nothing will kill a dream or douse the fire of a good idea more quickly than indifference. To whatever endeavor you commit yourself, be on guard primarily against that spirit-quenching attitude of apathy.

At what do you wish to succeed? A project? A job? A relationship? A personal mission? A financial goal? A life purpose? "Each one of us has a fire in our heart for something," says Mary Lou Retton. "It's our goal in life to find it and keep it lit."

In order to succeed greatly, one must care greatly. For indifference is no match against a well-attended fire in the heart.

Learning To Wait

You might remember comedian Yakov Smirnoff. When he first came to the United States from Russia, he was not prepared for the incredible variety of instant products available in American grocery stores. He says, "On my first shopping trip, I saw powdered milk – you just add water and you get milk. Then I saw powdered orange juice – you just add water and you get orange juice. And then I saw baby powder, and I thought to myself, "What a country!"

We live in a fast-paced world. We drive fast cars. We eat fast food. We live in the fast lane. We want it now.

One old story tells of a judge who was in a benevolent mood as he questioned the prisoner. "What are you charged with?" he asked. "Doing my Christmas shopping early," replied the defendant."

"That's no offense," said the judge. "How early were you doing this shopping?"

"Before the store opened," countered the prisoner.

Few of us will go to those extremes to satisfy our desire to "get it now," but we know what we want and we wish we could have it yesterday. We don't like to wait.

Though there is certainly a place for decisiveness and action, there is also a place for patience. Have you learned when to wait?

Wait for the sunrise...there will be another day.

Wait for guidance...learn to be still.

Wait for wisdom...it will come with experience.

Wait for growth...it happens in the fullness of time.

Wait and be contented...it is a secret to inner peace.

There is a time to act, but there is also a time to wait. Learn how to tell what time it is, for great things can happen for those who learn to wait. Ralph Waldo Emerson said it well: "Adopt the pace of nature; her secret is patience."

P.S.

It's not what happens to you; it's how you let it affect you.

The Only Answer That Really Matters

It's said that we begin to cut our wisdom teeth the moment we bite off more than we can chew. But do we ever feel as if we have enough wisdom? That we have arrived; that we are *wise*?

Jeff Hull writes about his great aunt, called Momma J. At 96, she was the last of her generation. As the family was gathered at her sister's funeral, a cousin remarked to Jeff that they were soon to be moving into the family's oldest generation. Jeff looked at his cousin and said plaintively, "But Mary, I don't feel like I know the answers yet."

After everyone had a good laugh, Mary turned to Momma J. and said, "When does that change, Momma?"

Momma J., from her wheelchair, smiled and said, "I don't know *yet*, dear."

Upon reflection, Jeff Hull asks this penetrating question: "How often do we let our own story about our limitations stop us from doing what we want to, what we are committed to, in life?" He is asking, "How often do we feel as if we have to know the answers before we can proceed, before we can follow our hearts, or before we can attempt something big?"

I like the wisdom of Sydney Harris. "Regret for the things we did can be tempered by time," he says, "It is regret for the things we did not do that is inconsolable."

You and I do not have all the answers yet. Truth is, we never will. But if we wait for all the answers, we will never move forward.

For no regrets, the only answer that matters is...take that next step. With courage, follow your heart's desire. The path ahead may be dark and hazy, for we can never see far into the future. But it is always clear enough to take one more step. And it's the way to a full and happy life.

P.S.

"In everyone's life, at some time, our inner fire goes out. It is then burst into flame by an encounter with another human being. We should all be thankful for those people who rekindle the inner spirit."

~ Albert Schweitzer

When Everything Is A Miracle

Marlin Perkins, long-time host of television's "Wild Kingdom," spent most of his life trying to put people on a first-name basis with animals. His wife Carol wanted to marry him so badly that she never let on that she did not fully share his passion for wildlife.

Soon after their marriage they went to central Africa. She tried valiantly not to complain during the long expedition, but one night she was exhausted. She said she wasn't hungry and just wanted to go to bed. So she undressed and reached for her pillow, when out from underneath crawled a huge lizard that ran up her chest and down her arm.

Carol started to scream and couldn't stop. She was so tired of being brave. Marlin came running, and after he saw that Carol wasn't hurt, he put his arm around her and said, "Honey, think of how lucky you were to see him up close."

I'm with Carol. I would find it difficult to appreciate the experience. But I am enthralled by Marlin's awe and enthusiasm for all things alive. He was able to marvel at the wonder of creatures and never lost his passion for animals. All living things, in their own way, were beautiful and splendid to this irrepressible lover of creation.

You may not choose to share your bed with a lizard, but do you find this world an exciting and wondrous place? Do you marvel at nature's handiwork? Do you want to "see it up close"? Does a spectacular sunset, the smell of seawater, that first spring flower, or the soft fall of snow soothe your soul? In short, are you excited about life and this magnificent world in which we live?

That amazing man Albert Einstein once said, "There are only two ways to live your life. One is as though nothing is a miracle. The other is as though everything is a miracle." But only one is the way of joy.

Your Work Is A Gift

Work sometimes has a bad reputation in our world. But there is something worse than work, and that is boredom. At least that is what Drs. Kathryn Rost and G. Richard Smith of the University of Arkansas say. After analyzing the mental health of heart attack survivors, they concluded that one factor which greatly reduced the chances of depression was going back to work.

And why not? At work we are often around friends, and people with strong relationships will almost always fare better mentally. But we humans also need to be useful and productive!

Arthur Kroeger wrote in *Quote* magazine (August 1994) that his brother sometimes visited an Anabaptist colony in southern Alberta, Canada. During one visit he asked leaders how they dealt with the problem of misbehavior – when people rebelled against the colony's strict rules. He was told that these people were first asked to correct their behavior. If they did not respond, they would be given a stern "talking to."

"But what do you do when all else fails, when somebody stubbornly refuses to behave?" he pressed.

"Ah," came the reply, "if it comes to that, then we don't give him anything to do."

The ultimate punishment – don't give them any work! If that doesn't sound so bad, just ask those who are unemployed how they feel about not working....

It has been wisely said, "The Lord didn't burden us with work, but rather blessed us with it." We *need* to be busy and productive.

Whatever it is you do to make a living – be grateful. Those long hours and that feeling of exhaustion at the end of the day come from having something useful to do. Your work is a gift. You are blessed.

P.S.

You can take no credit for beauty at sixteen; but if you are beautiful at sixty, it will be your own soul's doing.

Worry – The Real Enemy

What does it mean to worry? The Latin concept of worry describes a turbulent force within a person. Worry is a heart and mind in turmoil.

The ancient Greeks thought of worry as something that tears a person in two and drags that person in opposite directions. It is like opposing forces in deadly conflict within the very being of the individual.

The word "worry" itself comes from an old Anglo-Saxon term meaning to choke, or strangle, and that is exactly what it does – it chokes the joy of living wage right out of its victim. And it chokes off the energy to improve one's condition.

There is a place for healthy concern, but too often our concern turns into fearful worry. And worry, more than the problem, becomes our real enemy.

Some people have worried for so long that they have become *good* at it. Just as we can become good at any attitude or behavior if we practice it enough, we can also become good at worrying. Worry is habit – a habitual response to life's problems.

I rather like the attitude of the late United Methodist Bishop Welch. When he reached the age of 101, he was asked if he didn't think a lot about dying. With a twinkle in his eye, he replied, "Not at all! When was the last time you heard of a Methodist bishop dying at 101?" Maybe one reason for his longevity is that he never developed the habit of worry.

Next time you feel yourself worrying, be like the frogs – they eat what bugs them. Decide to no longer practice needless worry and instead practice peace. Replace your habit of fearful worry with the habit of courageous action. As Harvey Mackey has said, "Good habits are as addictive as bad habits and a lot more rewarding." Practice joy. Practice faith. And practice courage. Soon your life will be too rich and full for worry.

Celebrating You!

An old story tells of an unhappy and discontented stonecutter. One day he came upon a merchant and was awestruck by all of the marvelous goods the man had for sale. "I wish I were a merchant," said the stonecutter and, quite amazingly, his wish was granted.

Not long afterward he saw a parade pass his little shop. Spying a prince dressed in splendor such as he had never before seen, he said, "I wish I were a prince." And he became one.

But it wasn't too many days later that he stepped outside and felt the discomfort of the hot summer sun beating down upon his head. "Even a prince cannot stay cool in the sun," he said. "I wish I were the sun." This wish, too, was granted.

He was happy being the sun until, one day, a cloud came between him and the earth. "That cloud overshadows me," he said. "I wish I were a cloud."

Again, his wish was granted and he was happy until he came to a mountain that he could not rise above. "This mountain is greater than I," he said. "I wish I were a mountain."

As a tall and mighty mountain he looked down upon the affairs of humans and felt that he was finally happy. But one day a stonecutter climbed up his side and chipped away at rock and there was nothing he could do about it. "That little man is more powerful than I," the mountain said. "I wish I were a stonecutter."

So the circle was completed and now the stonecutter *knew* that he would always be happy just being himself. He would never dress like a prince, shine like the sun nor rise as tall as a mountain, but he was happy to be who he was.

A sure way to unhappiness is to compare yourself to others. Like someone aptly said, "The grass may be greener on the other side of the fence, but it still has to be mowed." You are who you are and that is to be celebrated.

P.S.

Why do tourists go to the tops of tall buildings and then put money into telescopes so they can see things on the ground close up?

Faith At Work

It's one thing to goof. But it's another thing to do it in front of a stadium full of people! In their book *Oops* (The Rutledge Press, 1981), authors Richard Smith and Edward Decter tell of such slip-ups. One occurred during a soccer match between two Brazilian teams. (To protect the player involved, I won't name the teams.) The first goal was scored within three seconds after kickoff. What made the score particularly hard for the team's fans to take was the fact that it was made while their goalie was still on one knee with head bowed in prayer.

There is certainly a time for prayer, but this poor man learned the hard way that there is also a time for action. In fact, both are necessary in a well-lived life. As Gandhi once said, "I have so much to accomplish today, I will have to meditate two hours instead of one."

Often, however, the best spirituality begins with the prayer of the heart, and then moves to that prayer which is lived throughout the rest of the day.

Several years ago a bomb was detonated outside the huge oak doors of a Greek Catholic church in Jerusalem. The heavy doors were blown inward so that they careened up to the front of the sanctuary and destroyed the chancel area. Windows were blown out, pews were destroyed, and the balcony collapsed.

Dr. Ken Bailey, a Presbyterian missionary scholar and friend of the priest of the Greek Church, stopped by to assess the damage. It took little time to determine that the priest was in shock and unable to make necessary decisions. So Dr. Bailey took it upon himself to ask seminary administrators at the school where he taught to close classes, and he invited students to join him in helping the priest. They cleaned the church and boarded the windows to prevent looting.

The next day, Bailey again called on his friend. The maid confided in him that the priest did not cry at the bomb's destruction. However, she added, "He did cry when you and your friends helped clean up the mess it made."

Dr. Bailey has since remarked, "I did not teach any theology that afternoon – or did I?" If theology is about love in action, he held one of his best classes that day.

The truth is...faith is never so beautiful as when it has its working clothes on.

When Life Gives You A Kick

I'm told the story is true: A woman was giving birth to a baby in an elevator at a hospital. When she complained about the location, a nurse said, "Why, this isn't so bad; last year a woman delivered her baby out on the front lawn."

"Yes," said the woman on the floor, "that was me, too."

Who said, "If I didn't have bad luck I wouldn't have any luck at all?" But on the other hand, not all "bad luck" should be considered a bad thing! Like someone said, "When life gives you a kick, let it kick you forward."

In the 1920s, Ernest Hemingway learned something about "bad luck" and getting kicked by life. He was struggling to make his mark as an author when disaster struck. He lost a suitcase containing all his manuscripts – many stories he'd polished to jewel-like perfection – which he'd been planning to publish in a book.

According to Denis Waitley in his book *Empires of the Mind* (William Morrow and Company, Inc., 1995), the devastated Hemingway couldn't conceive of redoing his work. All those months of arduous writing were simply wasted.

He lamented his predicament to friend and poet Ezra Pound who called it a stroke of good fortune! Pound assured Hemingway that when he rewrote the stories, he would forget the weak parts; only the best material would reappear. He encouraged the aspiring author to start over with a sense of optimism and confidence. Hemingway did rewrite the stories and eventually became a major figure in American literature.

Don't pray for fewer problems; pray for more skills. Don't ask for smaller challenges; ask for greater wisdom. Don't look for an easy way out; look for the best possible outcome.

When life gives you a kick, let it kick you forward.

P.S.

"Half the world is composed of people who have something to say and can't and the other half who have nothing to say and keep on saying it."

~ Robert Frost

A Mountaintop View

A police car pulled up in front of an older woman's house, and her husband climbed out. The polite policeman explained that "this elderly gentleman" said that he was lost in the park and couldn't find his way home.

"How could it happen?" asked his wife. "You've been going to that park for over 30 years! How could you get lost?"

Leaning close to her ear so that the policeman couldn't hear, he whispered, "I wasn't lost – I was just too tired to walk home."

These bodies become less cooperative as we age. For some, work becomes less fun and fun becomes more work. One older friend commented, "I've reached the age where the warranty has expired on my remaining teeth and internal organs."

But I like the spirit of Charles Marowitz. "Old age is like climbing a mountain," he says. "The higher you get, the more tired and breathless you become. But your view becomes much more extensive."

Atop the mountain, one has a better view of the world. One can see above the differences that divide people. One can better see beyond petty hurts and human fragility. Atop the mountain, one has a longer view of the past and can therefore understand the future with more clarity. Atop the mountain, one looks down on dark clouds of gloom and despair and fear and notices that they are neither as large nor as ominous as those beneath them would believe. It is also clearer that however dark they may appear, they too, are fleeting and will someday pass.

George Bernard Shaw said, "Some are younger at seventy than most at seventeen." I think it is because they have a broader outlook.

It will take a lifetime to climb the mountain, but, for me, the view will be worth the journey.

What We Really Want

What do you *really* want for the holidays?

USA Today printed these letters from children written to Santa Claus and directed to the US Post Office:

Dear Santa: The only wish I want is to have a nice Christmas for my little brothers. We don't have the money to put nothing under the tree because of welfare. Please help. There are five kids and it's hard for Mom. – Lisa

Dear Santa: I want to help the kids that don't get anything for Christmas. It is real important to me. I don't want just to help in the United States but all over the world. – Austin

Dear Santa: We will give you lots of goodies. One present is to find my dog Boom Boom. – Joni

Dear Santa: This Christmas I would like four things. Understanding for the children. Respect for the parents. Love for the elders and peace for everyone. – Rebecca

What these children *really* want runs deeper than the latest toy fad or a new outfit. I believe they want what we all want, when we get down to it.

I'm reminded of a story that comes out of World War I. It was December 25, 1917. Only a short distance of mud separated two enemy trenches – German and American. They had been shooting at each other for days, but today their thoughts turned to hearth and home.

Suddenly, a German soldier laid down his rifle, pulled a block of chocolate from his pocket, and tossed it into the American trench. In response an American tossed over a can of milk. Soon gifts were being passed back and forth, and the men were both laughing and weeping.

Peace was what they *really* wanted at that sacred time of the year. They wanted the war to be over and to be home.

They wanted to quit the fighting and violence and live in harmony. What they really wanted was what we all want.

I'll never stop believing that it can be so.

P.S.

Some people find fault like there was a reward for it!

Be Still

I have noticed that the best way for me to get a few minutes of solitude at the end of the day is to start washing the dishes. And a few minutes of solitude is something I need frequently. A time to be alone. A time to reflect.

There is a difference between aloneness and loneliness. Aloneness is necessary for the soul to thrive – even to come alive!

German theologian and pastor Dietrich Bonhoeffer was arrested and eventually hanged for opposing Hitler. While in prison, he wrote letters to his fiancée. The last letter she received was dated Christmas 1944. Speaking of the war that separated them, Bonhoeffer wrote this:

"These will be quiet days in our

homes, but I have had the experience over and over again that the quieter it is around me, the clearer do I feel a connection to you. It is as though in solitude the soul develops senses which we hardly know in everyday life. Therefore I have not felt lonely or abandoned for one moment."

We can be alone without being lonely. In fact, those times of solitude are necessary respite for our beleaguered souls, set upon by the pressures of life. We need to take those moments to "get away" and just be still. "Only in quiet waters things mirror themselves undistorted," says Hans Margolius. "Only in a quiet mind is adequate perception of the world."

Be still....

The Danger Zone

Anger is just one letter short of danger – it's true in English as well as in practice. Dr. Bedford Williams at Duke University has determined that students who scored high on a "hostility test" were in far greater danger of dying young than their peers. In fact, those who were prone to anger were in greater physical danger than those who smoked, had high blood pressure or even high cholesterol.

Not that we should never be angry. It is a normal part of life. We all get "worked up," "overheated" or just plain "hopping mad" at times. Those closest to us know it best. Like one little boy said, referring to his mother: "When she starts to act real weird, you have to look scared and serious. Don't giggle. When mommies are mad, they get madder when you giggle."

Getting angry does not seem to be the problem. Well-directed anger can be a helpful emotion. But staying angry is dangerous.

Here are four simple steps to move you out of the danger zone when you feel as if your hostility is managing you, rather than the other way around.

1. Control it. Uncontrolled anger will control you.
2. Talk it out. Don't keep it in and let it fester.
3. Act on it. Do what needs to be done to resolve the situation. Helplessness will only provoke more anger and, eventually, despair.
4. End it. Just as there was a starting point for your anger, there must be an ending. Make a decision not to prolong destructive hostility and you will find yourself healthier and happier.

For every minute you're angry, you lose sixty seconds of happiness. Are you ready to find peace?

P.S.

"It takes but one positive thought when given a chance to survive and thrive to overpower an entire army of negative thoughts."

~ Robert H. Schuller

Getting It Right

A young boy was sitting in the back seat of the car eating an apple. He poked his father in the front seat and asked, "Daddy, why does my apple turn brown?" His father answered, "When the skin is removed from the apple, air reaches the flesh of the apple and causes oxidation. This changes the apple's molecular structure and results in a brownish color.

After a long pause, a small voice from the back seat asked, "Daddy, are you talking to me?"

Too often I feel like that boy! I want answers. I want solutions to those confusing problems I run up against. I want someone to explain how to get through the difficult times and complex problems so that I can get it right! But I think I identify a bit more with the father whose daughter asked him if he would help her with some homework.

"I'm sorry," he replied. "It wouldn't be right."

"Well," she said, "at least you could try."

I don't have that many answers. And hard as I try, I can't ever get it all "right." But one of the most wonderful answers I *do* have is this: I don't *have* to always get it right! I don't always have to know what to do in every new situation I encounter. All I am required to do is give it my best, learn from the experience and go on.

The affable Dr. Leo Buscaglia once said, "No one gets out of this world alive, so the time to live, learn, care, share, celebrate, and love is now." Which is pretty hard to do when you're waiting for the answers first.

So you got it *wrong*! So what? Forgive yourself and try again. For even if you won't get out of this world alive, you *can* get life – joyful and abundant – out of this world.

Moments To Remember

We do not remember days, we remember moments.

In their book *Spiritual Literacy* (Touchstone Books, 1998), authors Frederic and Mary Ann Brussat tell about Oggie Rand. He manages a cigar store in Brooklyn. Oggie has an unusual habit – at precisely eight o'clock each morning, he photographs the front of the store from exactly the same spot. He collects his daily snapshots in photograph albums, each labeled by date. He calls his project his "life's work."

One day Oggie showed his albums to a friend. Flipping the pages of the albums, the man noticed in amazement that the pictures were all the same! Oggie watched him skim through the pictures and finally replied, "You'll never get it if you don't slow down, my friend. The pictures are all of the same spot, but each one is different from every other one. The differences are in the detail. In the way people's clothes change according to season and weather. In the way the light hits the street. Some days the corner is almost empty. Other times it is filled with people, bikes, cars and trucks. It's just one little part of the world, but things take place there, too, just like everywhere else."

This time Oggie's friend looked more carefully at each picture. No two were alike. He slowly became aware of how unique every moment is. Through a series of photographs, he became conscious of one of life's great truths – that each minute that passes is special, even sacred!

Writer Henry Miller has said, "The moment one gives close attention to anything, even a blade of grass, it becomes a mysterious, awesome, indescribably magnificent world in itself." But we'll never get it if we don't slow down. For it is these moments – not whole days, weeks, months or years – that we will finally remember. Whatever happiness and joy is to be found in life will be found in the moments.

Pay as close attention to each moment as you can, as if you were carefully observing a series of snapshots. Don't rush through them, allowing your mind to jump so far ahead that the present is lost. Each is unique. Each is sacred. And each holds a special place in time. In the end, it is these moments you will cherish and remember.

P.S.

Love many, trust few, but always paddle your own canoe!

Your Face Value

Ted Engstrom in *High Performance* (Here's Life Publishers, 1988) tells the story of a trusted advisor of President Abraham Lincoln who recommended a candidate for Lincoln's cabinet. Lincoln declined and when asked why, he said, "I don't like the man's face."

"But the poor man is not responsible for his face," his advisor insisted.

"Every man over forty is responsible for his face," Lincoln replied, and the prospect was considered no more.

Lincoln, of course, was referring to the man's expression and disposition rather than his features. A face conveys the thoughts and attitudes nurtured in a mind. We are responsible for how we will "face" each day.

One woman reported that she had just paid for some purchases when she heard the cashier say something. Not understanding, she asked her to repeat it. "I said have a happy day," the cashier snapped. "Are you deaf?" Here is a person who seems to be unaware of how she is facing others.

Earl Nightingale put it like this: "Our attitude is something we can control. We can establish our attitude each morning when we start our day. In fact, we do just that whether we realize it or not."

You are already choosing your attitudes every day. Your ultimate happiness or misery depends as much on your disposition as on your circumstances.

Face the day with hope and confidence, generosity and love, and you'll find yourself choosing to be happy. And you may be surprised at how much others like your face!

Four Traits Of Effective Leaders

A young officer in the Army discovered that he had no change when he tried to buy a soft drink from a vending machine. He flagged down a passing private and asked him, "Do you have change for a dollar?"

The private said cheerfully, "I think so. Let me take a look."

The officer drew himself up stiffly and said, "Soldier, that is no way to address a superior. We'll start all over again. Do you have change for a dollar?"

The private came to attention, saluted smartly, and said, "No, sir!"

Each of us commands some authority. There are or will be those we guide, supervise, rear, mentor or lead. Some of us will be effective and others will feel as if we're running a cemetery: we've got a lot of people under us and nobody's listening.

Much has been written and taught about leadership, but I find that at least four traits are common in all people of authority who effectively elicit cooperation and respect from those who look up to them. Whether you are a parent, whether you find yourself in the workplace, sitting on a volunteer committee or teaching someone a new skill, these traits will help you effectively guide those who would seek to follow.

These good leaders are...

Listeners. They take time to listen to the suggestions and concerns of those they endeavor to lead.

Encouragers. They don't try to do it all themselves. Neither do they motivate by force or guilt. They encourage others and help bring out their best.

Assertive. They say what needs to be said without being unkind. They tell the truth as they see it, openly and frankly.

Decisive. They know what needs to be done and they make timely, even difficult, decisions when necessary. But they can also take charge without running over the people in their lives.

In short, good leaders **L-E-A-D!**

It's said that the trouble with being a leader today is that you can't be sure whether people are following you or chasing you. But if you develop these four traits, your authority will be valued and respected.

P.S.

"The odds of going to the store for a loaf of bread and coming out with ONLY a loaf of bread are three billion to one."

~ *Erma Bombeck*

The Beautiful You

Our society places great emphasis on a narrow idea of physical beauty.

In an American history discussion group, the professor was trying to explain how, throughout history, the concept of "beauty" changes with time. "For example," he said, "take the 1921 Miss America. She stood five-foot-one inch tall, weighed 108 pounds and sported a 30-inch bust, a 25-inch waist and 32-inch hips. How do you think she'd do in today's version of the contest?"

The class fell silent for a moment. Then one student piped up, "Not very well."

"Why is that?" asked the professor.

"For one thing," the student pointed out, "she'd be way too old."

Good point – she'd be way too old. But beauty is a peculiar thing, for it means something different to each person. There are many kinds of beauty, and it isn't always about appearance. Authentic beauty is something deep within – the real you. For inside, you are more beautiful than you may ever know.

An elderly woman noticed that her granddaughter felt embarrassed by her freckles. "I love your freckles," she said, kneeling beside the girl and admiring her face.

"Not me," the child replied.

"Well, when I was a little girl I always wanted freckles," the grandmother said, tracing her finger across the child's cheek. "Freckles are beautiful."

The girl looked up. "Really?"

"Of course," said her grandmother. "Why just name one thing that's prettier than freckles."

The little girl peered into the old woman's smiling face. "Wrinkles," she answered softly.

She knew about beauty.

Believe It!

Writer Norman Cousins tells about a football game at which a doctor found himself treating five spectators for stomach disorder. Each complained of nausea, dizziness and cramps. Upon checking, the doctor learned that all five had previously consumed soft drinks from the concession stands. In the interest of protecting public safety, an announcement was made to the crowd that it would be wise to forego drinks in the stadium because certain people were becoming ill.

By the third quarter of the game, 200 people were reporting the same symptoms. Fully half of them were taken to a nearby hospital. Later in the afternoon the doctor determined that his five original patients had eaten potato salad from the same delicatessen on the way to the game.

The potato salad, not the drinks, was apparently the culprit.

Word was spread and those who were sick immediately began to feel better. The fans taken to the hospital were sent home as their symptoms quickly disappeared. Which all goes to show the tremendous power of belief. What we believe to be true will often become true. And not only in matters of health.

The power of our beliefs will dramatically affect those important decisions we make. Like automaker Henry Ford said, "Whether you think you can or not, you are right." If you believe you will succeed or fail, you are probably right. If you believe strongly enough that something good or bad will surely happen to you, it likely will. And if you believe that your life can become no less than a beautiful work of art, your belief will make it so.

Mahatma Gandhi found this principle to be true in his own experience. "If I believe I cannot do something, it makes me incapable of doing it," the Indian leader said. "But when I believe I can, then I acquire the ability to do it, even if I did not have the ability in the beginning." Your belief has the power to marshal needed resources and attract people who can help. That belief, more than any other single factor, will bring about what you want in life.

Speaker Nido Qubein put it like this: "If you believe you can and believe it strongly enough, you'll be amazed at what you can do." Believe it!

P.S.

It now costs more to amuse a child than it once did to educate her father.

~ *Distressed Parent*

For Goodness' Sake

A doctor said to his patient, "You have a slight heart condition, but I wouldn't worry about it."

"Really, Doc?" the patient replied. "Well, if you had a slight heart condition, I wouldn't worry about it either."

Many people believe that most of the world is more or less out for themselves and that most people care little about the plight of others. I choose to believe that most people are basically concerned about others, even if they don't always know how to express it. That is perhaps why a certain story, clipped years ago and filed away, has remained one of my favorites to this day.

A trucker relates that he was traveling through rural North Carolina on I-95 when a brown sedan merged onto the highway. It weaved back and forth between lanes, causing the driver of the truck to shift into a lower gear. At first he thought the driver was drunk, but when he came closer, the trucker saw an old man shaking uncontrollably behind the wheel. He noticed a Citizen's Band aerial whipping to and fro as the car jerked between lanes, so he called on the radio: "You in the brown Chevy, if you can hear me, pull over. Pull off the road!"

Amazingly, he did! The trucker pulled up behind the car and climbed from his cab. The elderly man staggered from his auto and fell into the trucker's arms. He poured out a story of months of fear and pain that accompanied the illness of his only daughter.

Now he was returning from the hospital where it was decided that she would cease any further treatment. In the hospital he remained "strong" and stoic for his daughter, but out on the road he fell apart.

The two men talked for the good part of an hour. The father eventually decided to share his pain with his daughter and said he felt good enough to drive home. The men embraced and the trucker followed him for 50 miles. As they drove along, the two talked together on the radio.

The older man finally acknowledged that his exit was ahead and thanked his new friend again for the help. The trucker asked if he could make it home all right and, suddenly, a third voice broke in on the conversation: "Breaker 19, don't worry, good buddy. Go your way. I'll see him home!"

Glancing in his rearview mirror, he saw a livestock truck move into the exit lane behind the brown sedan.

There are good people the world over. Some may be strangers to you, some as close as your own family. It helps to know that the world is full of people who will gladly give that caring touch, a needed warm embrace or a patient and listening ear. They are like angels who lift us to our feet when our wings have trouble remembering how to fly.

Look around, for they are everywhere. And quite likely, you will even spot one in the mirror!

Ruts And Graves

The difference between a rut and a grave is only a few feet! We like routine, but change is often necessary. Especially when an attitude or a behavior is standing in the way of a happy life. "If only I could change this about me..." we may lament.

The expression "turning over a new leaf" refers to the page of a book. Just as the plot of a novel changes from page to page, people, too, *can* change their lives! It is not only possible, but frequently necessary.

Why have so many ancient cultures died? What happened to some of the world's great civilizations, once alive with colors, people, music and ideas, that they are nothing more today than a collection of stones visited by tourists and historians?

The answer, of course, is not the

same the world over. But Arnold Toynbee, in his work *The Study of History* (Oxford University Press, 1987), says that the great lesson of history is this: civilizations that changed when confronted with challenges thrived. Those that did not change died. The key to survival is primarily about "change."

And what about us? What about you and me? It's good to accept ourselves as we are, but when an unhealthy attitude or a destructive behavior gets in the way, when we wish we could change something about ourselves, we had better change. People who embrace change thrive; those who resist it die.

If you have been waiting for a sign to make that needed change, this may be it. George Eliot said, "It is never too late to be what you might have been...." You *can* be happy. You *can* live fully.

Entrepreneur Brian Tracy said, "Resolve to be a master of change rather than a victim of change." Begin making that necessary change today. Then tomorrow, and every tomorrow thereafter, will truly be different.

P.S.

Life is like a rainbow. You need both the sun and the rain to make its colors appear.

Leafage And Rootage

American President Woodrow Wilson once pointed out that "a man's rootage is more important than his leafage." What others see are the leaves, the outside. What they can't see are the roots, the values and principles that ground a person. Character is grown from a good system of roots.

No one believed in the solid "rootage," the character, of President Jimmy Carter more than his own mother, "Miss Lillian." She was aware of her son's reputation for honesty, which had become a topic of curiosity among many politicians and even reporters. During a 1986 speech at the University of Tennessee, Jody Powell told a story about a television reporter who grilled Miss Lillian on this topic. "Is it true," asked the reporter, "that your son doesn't lie? Can you tell me he has never told a lie?"

"Well, I reckon he might have told a little white lie now and then," replied Miss Lillian.

The reporter spotted the opening. "I thought you said he didn't lie!" she exclaimed. "Are you telling me that white lies aren't as bad as black lies? Just what do you mean by a white lie?"

"Well," drawled Miss Lillian, "do you remember when you came in this morning and I told you how nice you looked and how glad I was to see you...?"

Jimmy Carter tried to develop a strong and principled inner life. That is what character is about. People of character live from the inside out. Their convictions guide their actions. Their principles govern their lives.

People of character have both the strength and grace to give their best to the world.

To their enemy they give forgiveness.
To an outsider, understanding.
To a friend, their heart.
To their children, a good example.
To their mates, faithfulness.
To their parents, respect.
To themselves, gentleness.

To all people, kindness.

Strong roots produce a strong character. And a strong character is needed to give one's best to life. When the tree's roots are well tended, the leaves will be full and healthy.

A Child Within

It was an annual winter tradition. Every year we packed the children into our family car and spent the day at "The North Pole at Pike's Peak," a year-round Christmas resort not far away. And each year they took turns on Santa's lap while we snapped pictures.

This wasn't any ordinary Santa, either. Maybe it was the *real* beard. Or maybe it was the twinkle in his eyes when he talked to our kids. Or maybe it was the warmth that could only radiate from the genuine Santa. But this kindly old man was Santa Claus at the resort all year round and, for our family at least, he was the real thing.

One year, after we finished with pictures, I said to him, "You must really love children."

"Yes, I do," he said. "And adults, too.

Many adults want to sit on Santa's lap for a picture!"

"Do you really have adults come to visit Santa?" I asked in amazement.

"Oh, yes," he replied. "As a matter of fact, one day 14 of the first 20 people who came to visit Santa were adults. All of us have a child inside of us. It's a terrible thing when you lose that."

I think I know what he meant. Children are enthusiastic. They've not forgotten how to have fun. And they still feel awe and wonder and...mystery.

"It's a terrible thing when you lose that," he said. I don't think he meant that we are to be childish and immature. Rather, childlike. Fun loving and ready to embrace life and love. Children are not yet jaded by exhausting problems or cynical about people. They know there is plenty about this universe they do not completely understand, and the mystery is likely to fill them with more awe than doubt.

Several years later, I had the honor of speaking at this Santa's funeral service. We remembered him as a man who always kept his childlike sense of enthusiasm about life. I'm sure he was one of the youngest old men to ever die.

Writer Randall Jarrell said, "One of

the most obvious facts about grown-ups to a child is that they have forgotten what it is like to be a child." Santa never forgot. I hope I don't, either.

P.S.

Sometimes you've got to wade through the mud to get to the river.

It's A Choice

One man tells of driving a long and lonely road, the last 65 miles of it unpaved, in order to watch Hopi Indian ceremonial dances in Arizona. After the dances, he returned to his car only to find that it had a flat tire. He put on the spare and drove to the only service station on the Hopi reservation.

"Do you fix flats?" he inquired of the attendant.

"Yes," came the answer.

"How much do you charge?" he asked.

With a twinkle in his eye, the man replied, "What difference does it make?"

This is what has been called a "Hobson's choice." A Hobson's choice is a situation that forces a person to accept whatever is offered or go without. According to Barbara Berliner (*The Book of An-*

swers, Simon & Schuster Inc., 1990), the phrase was inspired by sixteenth-century entrepreneur Thomas Hobson, who hired out horses in strict rotation at Cambridge University. There was no choosing by the customer – it was strictly Hobson's choice.

But most of the time we really *do* have a choice, and the choice we make *does* make a difference. We may not always believe it. We may feel as if we have no choice...we *have* to do such and such.

But we usually do have a choice. When we realize that most of what we do we do by choice, then we are taking control of our own lives.

Here is an experiment. For the next 48 hours, eliminate the words "I have to" from your vocabulary and substitute the words "I choose to." Don't say, "I have to work late tonight." Instead, say, "I choose to work late." When you choose to do it, you take control of your life. Instead of saying, "I have to stay home," try "I choose to stay home." The way you spend your time is your choice. You set the priorities. You are responsible. You have control.

There is very little in this life we *have* to do. You and I choose to do certain things because we believe that it will be for the best. When we eliminate "I have to" from our vocabularies, we take control. Try it for two days (after all, it's your choice), and you are sure to feel less help-less and more in charge of your life right away.

In almost every situation, we do have some choice. And the choice we make *will* make a difference. Take control – for in the end, it's those choices we make that will make our lives happier and more fulfilled.

Fully Committed

You may have heard the story about the world's most dedicated fisherman. He had out-fished his companion all morning long. They used the same live bait, the same equipment and fished together in the same mountain stream. But he had almost caught his limit of fish while his friend had yet to catch even one.

"What's your secret?" asked the friend. "I haven't even gotten a bite!"

The angler mumbled an unintelligible answer, causing his companion to ask again.

The successful fisherman emptied the contents of his mouth into a cupped hand and replied: "I said, You have to keep your worms warm."

That's commitment! But did you know there are at least three types of fishermen? First, there are those who fish only for sport. They usually "catch and re-lease," quickly throwing their catch back into the water.

Then there are those who fish because they like the taste of fish. They are selective. They only keep those fish they will someday eat.

Finally, there are those who fish in order to eat. If they don't succeed in catching fish, they skip a meal. It is this group of people who are most likely to succeed, for they approach their task with earnest dedication.

Whether or not we fish or even eat fish, the lesson is the same. We are most likely to succeed at a particular endeavor if we approach it wholeheartedly. Especially if the task before us is difficult or there seems little likelihood of success. Whether we want to patch a relationship, build a new business, write that first novel, kick a drug habit, or go back to school, we must decide if our task is important enough to commit to it. "Always bear in mind that your own resolution to succeed is more important than any other one thing," said Abraham Lincoln. For often, we will succeed only after we have fully resolved to do something.

The question we should ask ourselves is, "Just how much do I want this?" For not every job we do or task we attempt is worthy of complete dedication. We may choose to give lesser priorities less attention in order to give more of ourselves to those greater causes.

Other questions to ask are: "How will it affect me if I fail at this thing?" and "Am I willing to be fully committed in order to succeed?" For only in the dictionary does "success" come before "work."

Remember, when you are fully committed, the impossible can happen.

P.S.

The night is made to dream; the day is an opportunity to live those dreams.

From The Heart

Columnist Erma Bombeck once said, "It seems rather incongruous that in a society of super sophisticated communication, we often suffer from a shortage of listeners." Perhaps that is because many of us suffer from what communicator Nido Qubein terms "agenda anxiety" – the feeling that what we want to say to others is more important than what they might want to say to us. Sometimes we try to impress rather than express, not realizing that two monologues do not make a dialogue.

Relationships work when communication works. And communication works when we listen as well as speak; when we relate from the heart as well as the head.

In their book *Managing From The Heart* (Delacorte Press, 1990), the authors discuss what it means to communicate

from the heart. Here are five principles of
"H-E-A-R-T" communication:

Hear and understand me.

Even if you disagree, please don't make
me wrong.

Acknowledge the greatness within me.

Remember to look for my loving intentions.

Tell me the truth with compassion.

The quality of your life will be largely
determined by the quality of your relationships. And it is only with your heart that
you will communicate in ways that matter.

Connected For Life

Do you find yourself pulling away from others, especially if you've experienced a crisis or deep disappointment? We need other people and we'll never thrive as human beings in isolation.

A man who lost his wife to cancer found himself wanting to be alone. In time he dropped out of his worshipping community and curtailed all of the activities he and his wife had shared for so many years. He increasingly kept to himself. He quit socializing at work and returned straight home to an empty house. He turned down invitations from friends and co-workers. His leisure time was now spent watching television or working in his shop in the basement.

His contact with people dwindled until friends became alarmed that he might live out his life as a recluse. One came by to visit and to invite him over for supper the next evening. The two old friends sat in comfortable chairs by a warm fireplace. The visitor extended the invitation and encouraged him to allow others to share his pain. The man responded that he figured that he was better off without being around other people, who seemed to remind him of all he had lost. And besides, it was just too difficult to get out anymore.

They sat in silence for a while, watching the wood burn in the fireplace. Then the visitor did an unusual thing. He took the tongs from the rack, reached into the fire, pulled out a flaming ember, and laid it down by itself on the hearth. He still said nothing. Both men silently watched the red-hot ember lose its glow and turn slowly into a crusty, black lump. After some moments, the man turned to his companion and said, "I get the message, my friend. I'll be over tomorrow evening."

We cannot survive in any healthy way by ourselves. The leaf needs the branch. The branch needs the trunk. The trunk needs the roots. And the roots need the rest of the tree. We are connected. And in that connection we find life.

P.S.

Are you a thermometer or a thermostat? A thermometer only reflects the temperature of its environment, adjusting to the situation. But a thermostat initiates action to change the temperature in its environment.

Voice Of Compassion

I heard a story about Fiorello La-Guardia who was mayor of New York City during the worst days of the Great Depression and all of WWII. He was adored by many New Yorkers who took to calling him the "Little Flower," because of his name and the fact that he was so short and always wore a carnation in his lapel.

He was a colorful character – he rode the New York City fire trucks, raided city "speakeasies" with the police department, took entire orphanages to baseball games and, when the New York newspapers went on strike, he got on the radio and read the Sunday funnies to the kids.

One bitterly cold night in January of 1935, the mayor turned up at a night court that served the poorest ward of the city. LaGuardia dismissed the judge for the evening and took over the bench himself. Within a few minutes, a tattered old woman was brought before him, charged with stealing a loaf of bread. She told LaGuardia that her daughter's husband had deserted her, her daughter was sick, and her two grandchildren were starving.

But the shopkeeper, from whom the bread was stolen, refused to drop the charges. "It's a real bad neighborhood, Your Honor," the man told the mayor. "She's got to be punished to teach other people around here a lesson."

LaGuardia sighed. He turned to the woman and said, "I've got to punish you. The law makes no exceptions. Ten dollars or ten days in jail." But even as he pronounced sentence, the mayor was already reaching into his pocket. He extracted a bill and tossed it into his famous hat, saying, "Here is the ten dollar fine which I now remit; and furthermore, I am going to fine everyone in this courtroom fifty cents for living in a town where a person has to steal bread so that her grandchildren can eat. Mr. Bailiff, collect the fines and give them to the defendant."

The following day, New York City newspapers reported that $47.50 was turned over to a bewildered woman who had stolen a loaf of bread to feed her starving grandchildren. Fifty cents of that amount was contributed by the grocery store owner himself, while some seventy petty criminals, people with traffic violations, and New York City policemen, each of whom had just paid fifty cents for the privilege of doing so, gave the mayor a standing ovation.

Someone beautifully said, "Sympathy sees and says, 'I'm sorry.' Compassion sees and says, 'I'll help.'" When we learn the difference, we can make a difference.

At The Complaint Counter

I understand that an Athens hotel posts a sign that reads: "Visitors are expected to complain at the office between the hours of 9 a.m. and 11 a.m. daily." And you thought people didn't have to be told when to complain!

I do realize that all that is wrong in this world will not be fixed if it is not addressed. And there are those times when dissatisfaction should be expressed. I am also aware that we all have different temperaments. I just don't want to be one of those people who spend their lives "standing at the complaint counter"! Some people have taught themselves to look for what is wrong, and then they fill their minds and conversation with it. For them, nothing is ever right.

One such woman frequented a small antique shop. She complained constantly about the prices, the quality and even the location.

The shop owners took it in stride, but one day, while ranting about selection, she blasted the clerk with: "Why is it I never manage to get what I ask for in your shop?"

The clerk smiled and replied, "Possibly because we're too polite."

When a mind is filled with everything *wrong* about the world, there is no room left for anything else. No room for genuine appreciation. No room for understanding. No room for enjoyment. No room for fond memories. No room for storing a list of all the things that bring pleasure.

And there is much to feel good about! Bob Orben rightly said, "The next time you feel like complaining, remember that your garbage disposal probably eats better than thirty percent of the people in this world." I want to leave room in my mind for a long list of all that is good in my life and recall that list regularly. I want to catch someone doing something right and let her or him know. I want to fill my mind with that which brings me joy so that I may go to bed each evening contented.

"While others may argue about

whether the world ends with a bang or a whimper," says television producer Barbara Gordon, "I just want to make sure mine doesn't end with a whine." Now there's someone I'd like to get to know!

P.S.

If you have a hill to climb, waiting won't make it smaller.

Comp Time

Fulton Sheen once said, "Baloney is flattery laid on so thick it cannot be true, and blarney is flattery so thin we love it." There is a wide gap, however, between blarney and a sincere compliment.

Eleanor Roosevelt's mother, Anna, was deeply disappointed in her daughter's looks and demeanor. She often called young Eleanor "Granny." To visitors, she would say, "She is such a funny child, so old-fashioned that we always call her Granny."

"I wanted to sink through the floor in shame," an older and wiser Eleanor later recalled.

Adding to the cruel remarks, Anna told her young daughter, "You have no looks, so see to it that you have manners." Yet despite the obvious disappointment that Anna felt for her daughter, Eleanor forever wanted her mother's approval. Unfortunately, Anna died on December 7, 1892, at the age of 29, when her daughter was only eight.

At any age, sincere compliments and acts of appreciation feel like a warm fireside on a cold night. They melt away icy pain; they invigorate and refresh. We often remember them for years and they have remarkable power to influence future behavior.

One man lived by this motto: Never let a day go by without giving at least three people a compliment. It can give a whole new meaning to "comp time"! If you question the value of this exercise, give it a try. I think you will discover other people responding better to you, and you will experience a growing appreciation for the people in your life. And don't be surprised if, days or even years later, you learn how your words deeply affected someone in a significant way.

Remember, only three kinds of people respond well to a sincere compliment – men, women and children. Do you know any of these?

Secret Ingredient

There's a reason why some people succeed in life and others do not. Why some people seem to find their place while others never quite "get it together." And why many average and ordinary people accomplish extraordinary, or at least fulfilling, things while others expect that they will never really amount to much.

It is even more basic than raw talent or hard work. It is more fundamental than background or intelligence. It has to do with what makes successful people *use* the talent they possess or *choose* to work hard and persevere. It has to do with the reasons why some people compensate for poor backgrounds and others do not, why some intelligent people lead healthy and happy lives and others flounder.

In his article "How 'Average' People Excel" (*Reader's Digest*, 1992), Alan Loy

McGinnis tells about how Thomas J. Watson, Jr., discovered this "secret" ingredient to successful living and what happened to him as a result.

Watson's father was founder and longtime head of IBM. But young Thomas was a lackluster student who even needed a tutor to get through the IBM sales school. He recalls that he had no distinctions and no successes.

Then he took flying lessons. What a feeling! He learned that he was good at flying. He plowed everything into this "mad pursuit," as he fondly called it, and gained self-confidence.

Watson became an officer in the US Air Force during WWII. Though not brilliant, he discovered that he had "an orderly mind and an unusual ability to focus on what was important and to put it across to others."

He capitalized on these traits and went back to IBM. He eventually became chief executive of the corporation and took it into the computer age. In 15 years, he increased IBM's revenues almost tenfold.

What is it that some "ordinary" people possess and others lack? What is that ingredient that catapults some people up and away from the crowd? It is *confidence*.

"It's not what you are that holds you back," says entrepreneur Denis Waitley, "it's what you think you are not." Those who believe that they will never do well in a particular area probably never will. Those who believe they are not good at anything will forever feel inadequate. But those who refuse to let fearful thoughts hold them back will quickly excel.

Confidence is a life ingredient that is essential to success and wholeness. It is perhaps the single most important trait that enables "average" people to do and become all that they can.

Like the little boy sitting on the bench at his team's baseball game. When asked by a concerned parent if he was discouraged that his team was behind 14 to nothing, he responded, "Discouraged? Why should I be discouraged? We haven't been up to bat yet!"

With confidence like that, anything is possible!

P.S.

Stop worrying about the potholes in the road and enjoy the journey.

No More Problem!

One man exclaimed to his friend, "I just had another fight with my wife!"

"Oh, yeah?" the friend said. "And how did this one end?"

"When it was over," he replied, "she came to me on her hands and knees."

His friend looked puzzled. "Really? Now that's a switch! What did she say?"

"I think she said something like, 'Come out from under that bed, you gutless weasel.'"

Before your conflict escalates to that point, consider trying to solve your problem creatively. The novel, and sometimes humorous, approach is often the most effective!

A few years ago, I caught a story on the radio about a Baptist church that had a problem. It was with the Methodists down the street. Some Baptists were unable to find a space in their own parking lot because members of the nearby Methodist church, which met earlier than the Baptists, got there first. So the Baptist church had a problem.

Now, they *could* have towed the Methodists' cars away. Or they *could* have patrolled their lot Sunday mornings. Or they *could* have written a letter to the offending church members imploring them to park elsewhere. But they didn't.

Instead, they did something else. One Sunday morning they stuck a bumper sticker to every car in the lot – Baptist and Methodist alike. They all got one. The sticker read: *"I'm Proud To Be A Baptist!"*

No more problem.

Maybe that problem you are confronting will be solved more quickly and more effectively if you consider a more creative and humorous approach. What have you got to lose...except your ulcer?

The Work Of The Heart

For several years I have saved a touching piece written by teacher, Beth Nelson. She reminds us of the satisfaction gained by doing the "work of our hearts."

Let me give children the healing
knowledge
That there is a better way, a more
beautiful way
To live each day of their lives.
A physician I am not, but healing is
part of my profession.

Let me give some child hope for
eternity,
Peace in this life, confidence in what
will come.
I am not a member of the clergy, but
faith is part of my profession.

*Let me give children a feeling of
    justice,
A sensitivity for right and wrong;
A love of truth and abhorrence of evil.
A legal advisor I am not, but justice is
    part of my profession.*

*Let me bring children relief from pain
    of disappointment and disillu-
    sionment;
A remedy for dissolving personality;
An escape from the ravages of self-
    pity;
A psychologist I am not, but the
    healthy mind is part of my
    profession.*

*Let me give children a balance be-
    tween an appreciation of their
    cultural heritage,
And an enthusiastic participation in
    the human family,
And anticipation for the world of
    tomorrow.*
For I am a teacher.

To some, teaching may be a job; to
others, a means to a greater end. One person may think he merely lays bricks; another understands that he is helping to

build a hospital. Who among us cannot find a higher purpose in our work?

Michael Bridge beautifully says, "When our eyes see our hands doing the work of our hearts, the circle of creation is completed inside us, the doors of our souls fly open, and love steps forth to heal everything in sight."

P.S.

"Sprinkle joy."

> ~ *Ralph Waldo Emerson*

Victims And Fighters

Gretchen Alexander is sightless. But she refuses to allow her blindness to limit her life activities. She enjoys archery, golf, softball, sailing and water-skiing, as well as a number of other activities that those of us who are sighted have yet to learn.

She also speaks to groups about living life fully. When speaking to a group of high school students, she was once asked if there was anything she wouldn't try.

"I've decided to never sky-dive," she answered. "It would scare the heck out of my dog."

Why do some people rise above their problems and live life fully, while others become defeated? Merle Shain explains it this way: "There are only two ways to approach life, as a victim or as a gallant fighter. And you must decide if you want to act or to react...."

When discouraged, a victim reacts, perhaps in pain or self-pity. But a fighter acts. A fighter makes a decision to change that set of circumstances that left her or him discouraged. Or a fighter decides to accept those circumstances with grace and move ahead anyway. A fighter decides to act with courage. A fighter takes responsibility for his or her happiness. No matter how afraid, a fighter refuses to give in to the most defeating of all human emotions – helplessness.

A victim reacts. A fighter acts. It's your decision. It's a decision about whether you will live your life fully and with courage or whether you will be forever defeated by harsh circumstances. Make it well, for it may be one of the most important decisions you ever make.

Will you be a victim or a gallant fighter?

Uncommon Courtesy

A funny story has it that a police officer was investigating an accident. Referring to a woman lying unconscious in the street, he asked, "Who was driving the car?"

"I was," a man replied.

"How did you happen to hit her?" the officer inquired.

"I didn't!" he said. "As I approached the intersection, I saw that she was trying to cross the street. So I stopped for her and she fainted."

I'm not saying that courtesy is rare, but in some cities it's said that there are only two kinds of pedestrians: the quick and the dead. Maybe it's that "common courtesy" is not as common as it might be.

A wonderful story comes from 19th Century England. According to the account, Queen Victoria was once at a diplomatic reception in London. The guest of honor was an African chieftain. All went well during the meal until, at the end, finger bowls were served. The guest of honor had never seen a British finger bowl, and no one had thought to brief him beforehand about its purpose. So he took the bowl in his two hands, lifted it to his mouth, and drank its contents down!

For an instant there was breathless silence among the British privileged guests, and then they began to whisper to one another. All that stopped, however, when Queen Victoria silently took her finger bowl in her two hands, lifted it, and drank its contents! A moment later, 500 surprised British ladies and gentlemen simultaneously drank the contents of their own finger bowls.

It was the queen's uncommon courtesy that guarded her guest from certain embarrassment.

"Knowledge, ability, experience are of little avail in reaching high success if courtesy be lacking," says George D. Powers. "Courtesy is the one passport that will be accepted without question in every land, in every office, in every home, in every heart in the world. For nothing commends itself so well as kindness; and courtesy is kindness."

Call it what you may, courtesy is the one passport you can't be without if you intend to get where you want to go. Don't leave home without it.

P.S.

"Success is not the key to happiness. Happiness is the key to success. If you love what you are doing, you will be successful."

~ *Albert Schweitzer*

Saved By Criticism

One of my favorite stories comes from pilots Peter Gaylor and Stephanie Pound of Navajo Aviation. A funny thing occurred once when they flew their tiny airplane over the bay on an ash-scattering mission. With them were the two sons, in their twenties, of a late mother who was being consigned to the winds.

As Stephanie opened the cockpit door, a stiff breeze blew the ashes back into the plane, dusting the four occupants. A moment's stunned silence, and then one of the boys sighed, "Just like Mom – she was always all over everyone."

Maybe it was because she was their mother and believed it was her lot to correct. Children, especially, may feel that parents are "always all over them." Few of us particularly like others to point out areas for improvement. Dr. Norman Vincent

Peale said it well: "Most of us would rather be ruined by praise than saved by criticism."

I hold that encouragement is often more effective than criticism, and we should criticize sparingly. But those who are wise will regularly seek out someone they trust to hold a mirror before them that they may see themselves more accurately. It is important to know the truth, and it is often heard better when spoken by one who sincerely cares.

Someone accurately said, "Criticism, like rain, should be gentle enough to nourish one's growth without destroying one's roots." If you are in a position to critique, may your words nourish growth.

If you are the one reflected in the mirror, remember that what you see may be your salvation. Learn what you can and discard the rest. It may be more enjoyable to be ruined by praise, but what truth you hear will help you grow.

Not "Skeered Of Dyin'"

Economist Jeremy Gluck speculated on US Federal Reserve Board Chairman Alan Greenspan's epitaph. He decided it would probably read something like this: "I am guardedly optimistic about the next world, but remain cognizant of the downside risk."

Though many people feel at peace about their own eventual death, others are concerned about the possible "downside risk." One of humankind's greatest fears is around death and the process of dying. Like the song "Old Man River" says:

"Ah gits weary an' sick of tryin'.
"Ah'm tired of liven' an' skeered of dyin'."

Some people believe that the most basic of human fears is the fear of death. "Skeered of dyin'." Maybe you feel it, too.

In his later years, John Quincy Adams once remarked, "I inhabit a weak, frail, decayed tenement battered by the winds and broken in on by the storms, and from all I can learn, the landlord does not intend to repair."

Though he may have held out no hope that he would not die, he approached his own death with acceptance and a remarkable lack of concern.

When the elderly statesman fast approached his 80th birthday, he succinctly related his philosophy of death. The occasion happened as he hobbled down the street one day in his favorite city of Boston, leaning heavily on a cane, and a friend suddenly approached and slapped him on the shoulder.

"Well, how's John Quincy Adams this morning?" the friend inquired.

The old man turned slowly, smiled and replied, "Fine, sir, fine! But this old tenement that John Quincy lives in is not so good. The underpinning is about to fall away. The thatch is all gone off the roof, and the windows are so dim John Quincy can hardly see out anymore. As a matter of fact, it wouldn't surprise me if, before the winter's over, he had to move out. But as for John Quincy Adams, he never was better...never was better!"

I have spent much of my life around death. I have sat with people as they died. I have listened to others relate near-death experiences. I have studied theology and am aware of what scriptures and religions say about life and death. And I have come to the conclusion that death is not to be feared. Moreover, when it is time for me to move out of this tenement in which I am housed, I want to look forward to it joyfully. I want to say, "I never was better...never was better!"

P.S.

When you come to the edge of all the light you know and are about to drop off into the darkness of the unknown, faith is knowing that one of two things will happen: there will be something solid to stand on or you will be taught how to fly. – Unknown

The Rocking Chair Test

How are you at making decisions?

Years ago, a city family bought a cattle ranch and moved to the wide-open country. After a month, friends visited the family in their ranch house. "What did you decide to name your ranch?" they inquired.

"Well," the husband replied, "I wanted to call it the Flying W and my wife wanted to name it the Suzy Q, but one of our sons liked the Bar J and the other preferred the Lazy Y. So we compromised and call it the Flying W/Suzy Q/Bar J/Lazy Y."

"I see," said the visitor. "And where are your cattle?"

"None of them survived the branding!" said the rancher.

You, no doubt, make better decisions than that. But what do you do when you have a particularly tough decision to make? What do you do when your options are not at all clear?

When faced with a difficult decision, one man relies on what he calls the "rocking chair test." He imagines himself as an old man, nearing the end of his life. As he sits and rocks on his porch and contemplates his life, he asks himself if this decision will have any meaning to him. Will he be proud or ashamed of his decision? How will this decision have affected the course of his life?

The "rocking chair test" helps him take a long view of his options. If any decision passes the test, then he knows that it was a good choice.

What decisions are you presently struggling with? Take the "rocking chair test" today and make a better decision for tomorrow.

To Walk In The Light

Jewish humor has it that a rabbi and a priest met at the town picnic and began their usual "kibitzing." "This baked ham is just delicious," the priest teased the rabbi. "You really should try some. I know it's against your religion, but I can't understand why such a wonderful thing should be forbidden. You just don't know what you're missing. You haven't lived until you've tried Mrs. Kennedy's baked ham. Tell me, when are you going to break down and try a little ham?"

The rabbi looked at the priest, smiled and said, "At your wedding."

Truth is light...wherever it is found. Only one sun shines in the noonday sky. Likewise, the source of truth is one, in whatever religion it is found. "We can easily forgive a child who is afraid of the dark," said Plato. "The real tragedy of life is when [we] are afraid of the light." Afraid of the truth. And afraid of one another.

At one time in history, the religions of the world feared each other. Later they tolerated one another. Still later, they began to work together. Someday, they may laugh together. When that day comes, we'll know what it is to walk in the light.

P.S.

Nice guys finish last...but they have the most people waiting to greet them at the finish line.

How Much Do You Yearn?

Christopher Morley has said, "There are three ingredients in the good life: learning, earning and yearning." And yearning can make up for a great lack in the other two.

In Daniel Steele's book, *I Am, I Can* (Fleming H. Revell Co., 1973), the author tells a heart-warming story about the power of yearning. He tells that Columbia University football coach Lou Little was stopped on campus and informed of the unexpected death of the father of one of his players. He agreed to break the news to the student, as he knew that the young man and his father were quite close.

Two days after he went home to attend the funeral, the student returned to campus and was back on the practice field. "What are you doing back so soon?"

asked the coach. "You could have taken a week or two...we would have understood."

"Coach," the young man said, "my father was buried yesterday, and the rest of the family is taking care of things. Coach Little, I've just got to play in that game tomorrow. That's why I came back today."

The coach reminded him that tomorrow's game was a critical game and he might not play at all since he wasn't a usual starter.

But the student pressed, "I know I haven't played much, Coach, but I'm asking you for a chance to play tomorrow. I've just got to play in that game."

After a moment's hesitation, Coach Little said, "Okay, son, tell you what. If we win the toss, I'll let you play on the receiving team, but I can't promise you more than that."

The next day Columbia did win the toss. That young man went into the game and played like he had never played before. In fact, he was playing so well that Lou Little decided to leave him in longer. He had an outstanding day and, largely because of his effort, Columbia won the game.

In the locker room, the coach asked

the student, "What in the world happened to you out there? You never played ball like that in your whole life. That's the best exhibition of football I ever saw. How in the world did you do it?"

"Well, Coach," the exhausted and exhilarated young man said, "you never met my father, did you?"

"No, I didn't." Little replied. "I knew you were very close to your father, and I saw you walking arm in arm across the campus on several occasions, but I never met him."

"Well, you see," the student said, searching for the right words, "for most of my life my father was blind – and today was the first day he was able to watch me play."

There are few qualities more vital than a strong yearning to do or be something. Earning and learning help, but your desire, your yearning, will take you over the top.

An admirer once exclaimed to President Theodore Roosevelt, "Mr. Roosevelt, you are a great man!"

"No," he replied, "Teddy Roosevelt is simply a plain, ordinary man – highly motivated." It was his yearning that set him apart.

The Beauty Way

I guess I'm likely to put anything in my body!

I love spicy foods and Mexican foods in particular. I've "treated" friends to my favorite homemade spicy dishes. A typical reaction to a dish bathed in my hot sauce goes like this: they smile and enthusiastically try a bite; their eyes open far too wide and they begin to sweat profusely and reach for the water to put out the flames in their stomachs; then, when voice and reason return, they nod and politely say, "Tasty." They usually don't come back.

One person commented, "I've heard of people who preach hellfire, but you're the only one I know who hands out samples."

Well, maybe it's not quite that bad, but I'm likely to eat most any kind of food.

And though I exercise regularly, my body is starting to tell me to be more selective in my diet. I like the woman who stepped off the scale and was asked by her husband what the verdict was. "According to the height table," she replied, "I should be about six inches taller."

But more important than the food we put into our bodies are thoughts we put into our minds. Thoughts of bitterness like, "*I hate* her!" Thoughts of despair like, "I'll never be happy again." Thoughts of fear like, "I could *never* do that!" And thoughts of worry, thoughts of greed and thoughts of self-loathing. A constant diet of these killer thoughts will destroy us long before cholesterol.

The Navajo people have an expression for this. They traditionally believe that how they fill their minds will shape their lives. So they want to fill their minds only with that which is good, harmonious and edifying. They speak of "thinking in the Beauty Way" – ridding their minds of all that is destructive and filling them with that which is good and peaceful. The Beauty Way is the way of love and contentment, peace and kindness, patience and courage.

What are you putting into your mind? James Lane Allen has said, "You are today where your thoughts have brought you; you will be tomorrow where your thoughts take you." Fill your mind with life-affirming thoughts and tomorrow will find you further along the Beauty Way.

P.S.

"You can easily judge the character of a man by how he treats those who can do nothing for him."

~ James D. Miles

The Right Decision

The airline pilot announced over the intercom, "Folks, I've got good news and bad news for you. The bad news is...we're lost. The good news is...we're making *great* time!"

It's too easy to live our lives like that, isn't it? Always a bit too busy. In a hurry to accomplish the day's tasks. Rushing around...but not clear exactly where we want to ultimately end up.

It's been provocatively said, "Millions long for immortality who do not know what to do with themselves on a rainy Sunday afternoon." The problem is...they know they would *like* to accomplish something important with their lives or they would *like* to make a certain income or they would *like* to be happy. But when it comes to making the journey toward those destinations, they feel stuck. In short, they are lost.

Author and speaker Danny Cox, in his book *Seize The Day* (Career Press, 1994), tells of a man who made a great success of his life in spite of tremendous hardships. The moment that ultimately turned this man's life around was when he sat down and asked himself four important questions:

1) What do I really want? He didn't want to just sleepwalk through life, nor look back someday and feel regret.
2) What will it cost? In time, money and commitment.
3) Am I willing to pay the price?
4) When is the best time to start paying the price?

Answer these four questions and you will be clear on the direction you want to take your life. *Commit* to these answers and you'll make great time.

Led Around By Your "Gotta Haves"

Two women who had just met at a health spa were talking about their life-styles and how they hope to stay healthy. One asked the other to detail her daily routine.

"I eat moderately," she replied, "I exercise moderately, I drink moderately, and I live moderately."

"Is there anything else you do?" her new friend asked.

"Yes," she said, "I lie extensively."

I sometimes say I subscribe to the precept that all things should be done in moderation. Trouble is, I often follow that principle in moderation, too.

Not that we should be overly rigid. But self-imposed discipline is an absolute necessity if we are to be in control of our lives. And success and happiness is simply not possible without inner control.

A few years back, two Tennessee convicts dug under a fence and escaped to freedom. Within hours they were recaptured and returned to prison, where they both had several years added to their sentences. Strangely enough, at the time they dug under the fence, one of the men would have been released in 30 days. He was asked why he risked extra years in prison when he could have been out in a month, and he replied, "I couldn't wait."

One hospital patient aptly described the problem. When visiting with a chaplain, this patient, who was being treated for venereal disease, said, "Reverend, my trouble is I've been led around by my 'gotta haves' all my life."

Self-discipline is vital to any successful and happy life. Without it, we're led around by our "gotta haves" all our lives. Whatever we think we gotta have this moment is what we follow. We gotta have more pleasure or less discomfort or this experience or that new thing or another glass.... You fill in the blanks.

On the other hand, happy and successful people usually feel in control of themselves. They are self-directed and self-disciplined. If they overdo, it does not become a lifestyle. If they deviate from the goals they've set, they soon get back on course. They know how to have fun without being led around by their gotta haves.

Writer Peter DeVries has said, "I write when I'm inspired, and I see to it that I'm inspired at nine o'clock every morning." He has learned that creativity, too, needs discipline.

I like the words of Bernard Baruch. "In the last analysis," he said, "our only freedom is the freedom to discipline ourselves." Discipline is deciding not to be led around by our gotta haves. It is the task of a lifetime, an indispensable prerequisite to success, and the only way to be truly free!

P.S.

"There is always music amongst the trees in the garden, but our hearts must be very quiet to hear it."

~ *M. Aumonier*

Not Just A Pipe Dream

Are your dreams and beautiful ideas just pipe dreams?

According to Webb Garrison in his book *Why You Say It* (Rutledge Hill Press, 1992), the term "pipe dream" has its origins in the 19th century. The drug opium was imported into Europe from Asia and was widely used in certain literary circles in Britain. Opium was smoked in a pipe and, once under the influence, people had hallucinations that were referred to as pipe dreams. So today, an unrealistic or impractical idea may be quickly discounted as a pipe dream.

But not all seemingly impossible or far-fetched ideas are merely pipe dreams. A case in point is the dream millionaire Eugene Lang gave to high school students in the impoverished neighborhood in which he was raised. Addressing a class of eighth-graders in the South Bronx, Lang threw away his prepared speech. The empty eyes of the students in attendance told him they were not interested in his "motivational" talk. Their neighborhood had become a battlefield of poverty, drugs and gangs, and a breeding ground of despair. About 80% of them would not complete high school. Few would ever leave the neighborhood. Fewer still would climb out of poverty. That is why Mr. Lang tossed aside his speech. The students didn't need a speech; they needed a dream.

Then, the words that came from Eugene Lang's mouth may have even astonished him! "If you graduate from high school," he told the youth, "I will send you to college." Send you to *college!*

For the next four years he worked with the school and kept the dream alive. And the results were phenomenal: all but two of the 60 teenagers finished high school! True to his word, he sent them to college. "He gave us hope," one student said, no doubt speaking for the majority. Another one of the students, upon meeting Lang later, said to him, "Mr. Lang, we did the impossible."

Not every seemingly unrealistic idea is a pipe dream. When that beautiful dream is combined with hard work and great expectation, then the impossible can be achieved. For when you believe enough in that magnificent dream, most anything can happen.

Way To Results

Melodie Hartline relates in *Reader's Digest* (September, 1996) that in her job as an employee of a jewelry store, she often arranged for engaged couples to have their wedding bands engraved with something special. She once asked a bride-to-be what she would like inscribed inside her fiancé's ring.

"We aren't very romantic," she replied. Then she related that they were marrying on her fiancé's birthday so he wouldn't forget the date!

Melodie persisted, "Isn't there something you'll want him to remember as he looks inside his ring?"

"There sure is," she said. And that's how "Put it back on!" came to be inscribed inside her husband's ring.

Perhaps she was trying to "help along" her husband's commitment to the relationship.

Catherine, from Scotland, may have wanted to help along her lover's commitment for several decades. And finally, her 68-year-old boyfriend, George, proposed after 44 years of courtship. Why the wait? "He is a bit shy, you know," Catherine said.

At the heart of any meaningful relationship is commitment. Further, commitment is vital to the success of any endeavor. Happy people are committed people. They commit to other people, they commit to themselves, they commit to God, and they commit to their dreams. They know that nothing is possible without firm resolve.

Author Ken Blanchard has said, "There's a difference between interest and commitment. When you're interested in doing something, you do it only when it's convenient. When you're committed to something, you accept no excuses - only results."

What about you? Are you ready for results?

P.S.

"You can't get where you're going while you're living where you've been."

~ *Dalton Roberts*

Getting An Education

Parents often complain to me about how long it takes their kids to complete college. It seems that most attend school now for many years, though not full time. I asked one father what his son was going to be when he graduated, and he replied, "An old man."

Mark Twain said this about his own education: "I never considered myself a slow learner. I always felt that teaching just came hard to most of my instructors." But formal education is only a part of the education of a lifetime. I have had my share of formal education, but most of what I know today has been learned outside the classroom.

Cindy, a subscriber of my daily Internet newsletter *Your Life Support System* (www.LifeSupportSystem.com), wrote that David Harp's book titled *The Three*

Minute Mediator (Fine Communications, 1999) contains a chapter on the Zen of "Don't Know." In it, he talks about the attitude required to learn throughout life. Harp tells a story of a scientist who visited a Buddhist teacher in order to learn about Buddhism from a "scientific" point of view. The Buddhist instructor suggested that, before they begin, they have a cup of tea. He filled the scientist's teacup to the brim. Then, after pausing for a second, he poured more tea into the cup. The scientist leaped up as the hot tea cascaded into his lap.

Thus began the first lesson: "A teacup that is too full," the Buddhist said, "can receive nothing additional. Neither can the mind."

Much can be learned when the mind is receptive (by the way, I have found scientists, as a group, to be quite open-minded). Your "life" education requires no acceptance into an accredited school – you're already enrolled in the school of Life. There will be no grades, but the success of your living will demonstrate how well you've learned. You will be assessed no fees for your education, for the price you pay is an open mind. A closed mind learns nothing. Finally, there will be no graduation ceremony, for your instruction continues all of your life.

As Ken Keyes has said, "Everyone and everything around you is your teacher." Look, listen and learn well. Your life depends on it.

Same Here!

One man was annoyed at his sentimental wife's constant sniffling as she watched a touching movie on the television. "For goodness' sake," he scolded, "why is it you cry about the imaginary woes of people you've never met?"

"For the same reason you yell and scream when a man you don't know scores a goal," she said.

That reason, of course, is that they identify with the person or the event. The word "identify" originally comes from the Latin root "idem," which means "same." When we identify with someone, we feel the same sadness or ecstasy the other feels and we understand another's plight.

There is no substitute for an ability to identify with others. One woman wrote me a letter about how she acquired this valuable trait. She said this:

"I was a registered nurse for quite a few years. I always thought of myself as an empathetic person, somebody who was able to reach out and understand what someone else was going through. Then I became a patient when I was diagnosed with M.S. and realized I never really knew the true meaning of the word "empathy." Unfortunately, it sometimes has to be learned and not taught.

"I found out just how much even a smile means to someone who is sick and so scared about what is happening in their life. [Because of M.S.], I found out how much it means to have someone take a few minutes and be friendly and just talk.... I hate the disease, but it has taught me so much!"

This woman had worked compassionately and professionally for years, but now there is a whole new dimension in her dealing with patients. She identifies with them. She *knows* how they must feel and responds differently. And she has become a better nurse (and person) because of it.

You may never treat hospital patients, but is there anyone in your life who would not benefit from your ability to identify with their pleasures and pains, their wild dreams and dashed hopes?

The ability to identify with others is a trait that, with practice, can be learned. Employers and employees are valued more highly when they possess it. Family and friends create more intimate relationships when those bonds are built around an ability to truly identify with one another.

Lord Chesterfield said, "You must look into people, as well as at them." It is a rare friend who has cultivated the ability to clearly see inside others and, thereby, identify with them. But it is a necessary part of an effective and happy life.

P.S.

"I'm not confused, I'm just well mixed."

~ *Robert Frost*

Pushers And Pullers

One woman tells of a time her dog disappeared. After searching diligently, she placed a "lost dog" ad in the local newspaper.

The following morning her phone rang and a weak, cracking voice began, "I'm calling about your dog." Then the caller coughed and cleared her voice a few times. She explained that she wasn't feeling well and that, in fact, she had not felt well since her husband's death three years ago. She went on to relate that her parents, too, had passed away since then and her sister was diagnosed with a fatal ailment. Even her friends, she continued, were not doing well, and she gave details of their various maladies and described the funerals of several of them.

After 30 minutes of listening, sympathizing and even trying offers of help, the dog owner steered the conversation back to the original subject. "About the dog," she began.

"Oh," the caller replied, "I don't have him. I just thought I'd call to cheer you up."

Maybe her technique needed refining, but her intentions were right on. And though "cheering up" may not be exactly what we require, we certainly need encouragement – pulling up – at times. A heartfelt word of encouragement will quench a spirit parched by affliction as surely as a cup of cool water will refresh a dry and thirsty throat.

The need for sincere encouragement is basic among human beings. The Smithsonian Institution in Washington, D.C., displays the personal effects found on President Abraham Lincoln the night he was shot. They include a small handkerchief embroidered "A. Lincoln," a pen knife, a spectacle case repaired with cotton string, a Confederate five-dollar bill, and a worn-out newspaper clipping extolling his accomplishments as president. The article begins, "Abe Lincoln is one of the greatest statesmen of all time...."

Why would one of the most highly regarded leaders of American history carry around such a document? Did he not know his own worth? The answer is found in the fact that Lincoln was not as popular during his lifetime as he became after death. His leadership was under constant fire, he was frequently an object of ridicule in the press, and bitter critics dissected his every decision. He needed something to remind himself that, though battered by the disappointments of life and scorned by those he sought to lead, there were still also others who valued his contribution. There were still those, perhaps not as vocal, who believed in him. He, too, needed encouragement.

Do you need encouragement? There are those who will rally to your side. Educator Booker T. Washington observed, "There are two ways of exerting one's strength; one is pushing down, the other is pulling up." There are people ready to pull you up when others are pushing down. We need those people in our lives; those who exert their strength by pulling us up.

I believe these people can be found everywhere. I believe that we can all become "pullers," lifting one another from dark pits of discouragement to the light of hope. And when that happens, the world will never be the same.

Live It!

Editor, diplomat and poet James Russell Lowell had a wonderful attitude. One day, when passing a building in the outskirts of Boston, he noticed an identifying inscription: "Home for Incurable Children." To a friend he remarked, "They'll get me in there some day."

If he means that he'll never be cured of an overriding enthusiasm for living, then I also hope they'll get me into a place like that some day. I never want to outgrow my zeal for life. I never want to become so jaded as to take living for granted.

Whoever compiled this list knew how to live with enthusiasm! Here's all the advice you'll need to live well and with zeal.

Life is beauty; appreciate it.
Life is a dream; realize it.

Life is a challenge; meet it.
Life is a duty; complete it.
Life is a game; play it.
Life is a sorrow; feel it.
Life is a song; sing it.
Life is a struggle; accept it.
Life is an adventure; risk it.
Life is luck; make it.
Life is a puzzle; solve it.
Life is opportunity; take it.
Life is a song; sing it.
Life is a mission; fulfill it.
Life is life; live it!

P.S.

*Happiness is wanting what you have,
not having what you want.*

A Wonderful Time

I have a collection of humorous and poignant epitaphs and tombstone verses. Not because I am morbid, but because what is said about someone who has recently died is so important. Granted, not all tombstone sayings are telling. Like the one for Lester Moore at Boot Hill Cemetery in Tombstone, Arizona:

Here lies Lester Moore
Four slugs from a 44
No Les
No More.

Or this grave marker from Union-town, Pennsylvania:

Here lies the body of Jonathan Blake
Stepped on the gas
Instead of the brake.

Sometimes these "last words" reveal more than the deceased may have wanted, like this one:

Here lies a fellow who lived for himself
And cared for nothing
But gathering pelf,
Now, where he is or how he fares,
Nobody knows and nobody cares.

These posthumous writings will often summarize a life. If accurate, they can point the reader to that which was most important to the deceased. Did this person enjoy life? Was she cared for? Did he make a difference? Did she leave a legacy?

When you die, how will you be remembered?

Columnist Nick Clooney in *Nick: Collected Columns of Nick Clooney* (Irena Hochman Fine Art Ltd., 1997) printed some epitaphs from people still alive, written by themselves. Some were humorous, some serious. Some hoped that their own original epitaph would be close to the way they might be remembered. One that I truly love came from Charlie Mechem, former head of Taft Broadcasting. Charlie wished that this might be put on his tombstone: "Dear God, Thanks for letting me visit. I had a wonderful time."

Isn't that terrific? And could it be said about you...that you were grateful for the visit and had a wonderful time? That's a life worth living!

Be A Good One

Pablo Picasso, the great Spanish painter and sculptor, once said this about his ability: "My mother said to me, 'If you become a soldier, you'll be a general; if you become a monk, you'll end up as Pope.' Instead, I became a painter and wound up as Picasso." No lack of confidence here!

But he would have agreed with Abraham Lincoln. "Whatever you are," said Lincoln, "be a good one." He demonstrated the wisdom of that advice with his own life. And in this present age, which often seems to be contented with mediocrity, his words summon a yearning for improvement and growth.

I think it helps to remember that excellence is not a place at which we arrive so much as a way of traveling. To do and be our best is a habit among those who hear and understand Lincoln's admonition.

Viennese-born composer Frederick Loewe, whom we remember from his musical scores that include "My Fair Lady," "Gigi" and "Camelot," was not always famous. He studied piano with the great masters of Europe and achieved huge success as a musician and composer in his early years. But when he immigrated to the United States, he failed as a piano virtuoso. For a while he tried other types of work including prospecting for gold and boxing. But he never gave up his dream and continued to play piano and write music.

During those lean years, he could not always afford to make payments on his piano. One day, bent over the keyboard, he heard nothing but the music that he played with such rare inspiration. When he finished and looked up, he was startled to find that he had an audience – three moving men who were seated on the floor.

They said nothing and made no movement toward the piano. Instead, they dug into their pockets, pooled together enough money for the payment, placed it on the piano and walked out, empty handed. Moved by the beauty of his music, these men recognized excellence and responded to it.

Whatever you are, be a good one. If what you do is worth doing, if you believe that who you are is of value, then you can't afford to be content with mediocrity. When you choose the path of excellence through this life, you will bring to it your best and receive the best it can offer in return. And you will know what it is to be satisfied.

P.S.

The biggest trouble with having the gift of gab is wrapping it up.

Greater Strengths

If you're like most of us, failure is not your best friend! But I like the attitude of one man. "I don't say I have strengths and weaknesses," he asserts. "I say I have strengths and lesser strengths." That's me! Lots of strengths...many of them "lesser strengths!"

One of my "lesser strengths" may be in the area of art. But when my three-year-old asked me to draw a picture of a horse on his chalkboard, I agreed anyway. And it wasn't too bad.... Well, it wasn't very good, either. It reminded me a little of a mongrel dog with hooves, but as they say, I've seen worse. (Actually, it was my own drawings that were worse.) And I felt pretty good about the picture when his preschool friend stopped by the house, looked in his room and said, "Who drew the horse?" I even felt a bit proud! So I proudly called down the hall, "I did!"

There was a moment of silence as a look of confusion swept her face. Then she asked, "Did you draw it when you were a baby?"

Everyone's an art critic!

But I'm thankful to my son's friend for reminding me about my strengths. Sure, I'd starve as an artist, but I don't have to excel at art. I have other strengths. And I can marvel at good art while I pursue my own strengths.

John Wooden said, "Don't let what you cannot do interfere with what you can do." There's nothing wrong with a list of things you are not able to do. These are just your lesser strengths. The key is to choose your greater strengths well. What is important to you? What *must* you excel at? And what *can* you do well? Focus on these priorities and your lesser strengths won't matter much.

But don't ask me for a picture of a horse.

A Life That Makes A Difference

"How do you account for your re-markable accomplishment in life?" Queen Victoria of England asked Helen Keller. "How do you explain the fact that even though you were both blind and deaf, you were able to accomplish so much?"

Ms. Keller's answer is a tribute to her dedicated teacher. "If it had not been for Anne Sullivan, the name of Helen Keller would have remained unknown."

Speaker Zig Ziglar tells about "Little Annie" Sullivan, as she was called when she was young. Little Annie was no stranger to hardship. She was almost sightless herself (due to a childhood fever) and was, at one time, diagnosed as hope-lessly "insane" by her caregivers. She was locked in the basement of a mental insti-tution outside of Boston. On occasion, Little Annie would violently attack anyone who came near. Most of the time she generally ignored everyone in her presence.

An elderly nurse believed there was hope, however, and she made it her mission to show love to the child. Every day she visited Little Annie. For the most part, the child did not acknowledge the nurse's presence, but she still continued to visit. The kindly woman left cookies for her and spoke words of love and encouragement. She believed Little Annie could recover, if only she were shown love.

Eventually, doctors noticed a change in the girl. Where they once witnessed anger and hostility, they now noted an emerging gentleness and love. They moved her upstairs where she continued to improve. Then the day finally came when this seemingly "hopeless" child was released.

Anne Sullivan grew into a young woman with a desire to help others as she, herself, was helped by the loving nurse. It was she who saw the great potential in Helen Keller. She loved her, disciplined her, played with her, pushed her, and worked with her until the flickering candle that was her life became a beacon of light to the world. Anne Sullivan worked wonders in Helen's life, but it was a loving nurse who first believed in Little Annie and lovingly transformed an uncommunicative child into a compassionate teacher.

"If it had not been for Anne Sullivan, the name of Helen Keller would have remained unknown." But if it had not been for a kind and dedicated nurse, the name of Anne Sullivan would have remained unknown. And so it goes. Just how far back does the chain of redemption extend? And how for forward will it lead?

Those you have sought to reach, whether they be in your family or elsewhere, are part of a chain of love that can extend through the generations. Your influence on their lives, whether or not you see results, is immeasurable. Your legacy of dedicated kindness and caring can transform lost and hopeless lives for years to come.

You can never overestimate the power of your love. It is a fire that, once lit, may burn forever.

Index

Index, cont.

Also by Steve Goodier

One Minute Can Change a Life
Riches of the Heart
Joy Along the Way
Prescription for Peace
Touching Moments
Lessons of the Turtle
The Living Right Side Up Method

Free shipping! Free gift-wrapping!

Please call toll free 1-877-344-0989
Or order from the Web site!
www.LifeSupportSystem.com

Get Steve Goodier's **FREE newsletter**
Your Life Support System.
www.LifeSupportSystem.com

"Sharing Life, Love and Laughter . . ."